Vintage France

Vintage French Decor Ideas

Copyright © 2023

All rights reserved.

DEDICATION

Contents

I. An Ever-Changing Serence

If you love vintage French design you'll love this home and you might even have seen the vintage book guide..

They are living in an ever-changing styling space/shop but it does create a wonderful home and it must be quite nice to constantly collect pieces and restyle your home. The result is a stunning light vintage home that feels extremely serene despite the many little decor items you'll see throughout the home.

Rooted in a rustic, warm base dressed with refined, elegant accents, French country decor offers the best of both worlds: a comfortable, lived-in home that's undeniably luxurious too. "It's a wonderful yin and yang," says Anita Joyce, author of _French Accents: Farmhouse French Style For Today's Home_, host of _Decorating Tips and Tricks_, and publisher of Cedar Hill Farmhouse. Though often described as a close relative of <u>farmhouse style,</u> country French decor still has its own aesthetic DNA. Eager to learn more? Here, *AD* chats with Joyce, along with Amitha Verma, an interior designer, founder of <u>Amitha Verma Furniture Paint,</u> and owner of Village Antiques in Houston (also known as Farmhouse by Amitha), all about this warm and graceful style.

Neutral color palettes are common in French country decor. Flowers and soft blue pillows add a pop of color.

What is French country decor?

According to Joyce, French country decor is "a relaxed take on Provence style, with a mix of rustic and refined elements." As she points out—and as the name implies—the aesthetic is inspired by the effortless, simplistic beauty of both the French countryside itself and the lifestyle that those who live in the region often embody. "It uses natural elements mixed with authentic French antiques," she explains. "I would call it a refined elegance where embellishments are tempered by natural elements and relaxed comfort." Like many things French, it feels effortless yet undeniably chic. "Picture if I were a gal living in Paris in a beautiful apartment, and I've been collecting these beautiful antiques, silk-covered bergères, gilt lamps, and antique commodes, and then one day, I decided to move out to the countryside, buy a farmhouse, and restore it." Verma says. "I take all of my beautiful antiques and I mix them into this very rustic home and a lifestyle where I'm dragging my boots with mud on them inside of my home. That's the look, all in one home."

Intricate carving and painted wood, as seen on these chairs and buffet, is a common element of French country decor.

What is the difference between farmhouse and French country?

While there are notable similarities between farmhouse style and French country decor, there are also many distinguishable differences. Perhaps the most obvious connection is their shared emphasis on rustic, homespun features. "All of the rustic elements are very similar," says Joyce. Both have old-world roots, but while a French country home is—obviously—inspired by the French countryside, farmhouse style is often inspired by American farms.

In Anita Joyce's dinning room, rustic elements, like a farmhouse-style table, meet daintier accents, like the chandelier.

While not exclusively true—and there are certainly overlaps—locales outside of large metropolitan areas in France often inspire images of rolling hills, cottages covered in climbing vines, and fields of colorful wildflowers. Farms—though again, not always true—are often allied with barns, fields of crops, and the stereotypical style of a farmer, things like denim, plaid, or even cowboy boots.

While both of these foundations influence the more rustic nature of these two design styles—think beamed ceilings and the use of natural materials—modern farmhouse style is often more utilitarian, with sharper lines and a more casual look. You'll often find heavier materials like brass or steel and elements like shiplap, reminiscent of barns, in this style of home. Country French style, on the other hand, uses this same baseline, but adds in daintier elements. "I think you could take a farmhouse room and throw in some French furniture and some antiques and then you would have French countryside," Joyce says. "But you've got to add in the refined elements and flourishments to the casual foundation." As Verma explains, understanding the history of French country decor can provide further context to what the style actually is, and how it compares farmhouse style. "It really boils down to the decade," she says.

History of French country decor

Patterns, like the plaid seen on Joyce's armchair, is a common ingredient in French country decor.

Back in the 1700s, France was ruled by King Louis XV, whose monarchy, intentionally or not, greatly influenced the French country style we know today. "Through the Napoleonic and even after, all of the interior design is influenced by the monarchy," Verma explains. During his rule, "he enjoyed taking his court to the countryside and enjoying many of the leisurely pursuits of life," she says. Of course, this helps contextualize why—and how—French country style honors both a rustic aesthetic and an elegant one. "From this time, this is where everything we know and love about the French country is born," Verma adds.

At the same time, the United States was a considerably younger country and didn't gain its independence from England until the late 1700s. As such, the more leisurely pursuits of life weren't the top priority. "So farmhouses were much more utilitarian, with simple, straighter lines and more vernacular design, meaning you just use whatever you have around you to create your structures and your furniture."

It's worth noting that French country decor doesn't necessarily "exist" in France. "They just call it farmhouse," Verma says. The specific name is often understood as a reflection of the United States trying to emulate this country lifestyle. As Joyce recalls, it first started to gain traction in the US around the '70s, though it was a simplistic view of that culture. "For lack of a better word, it wasn't very refined," she says. "I wouldn't call it super authentic." However, in the '90s, Charles Faudree reintroduced the style in a whole new way. "He's Mr. Country French," Joyce says. "He used all of these authentic elements, and I feel like he really kicked it up a notch." While Faudree perhaps took a more formal approach to the decorating style, as it evolved over the years, practitioners started to embrace the more casual elements of the style, but with touches of the authentic, refined look Faudree introduced. "I would say the updated version now has less color and more muted tones with simplistic patterns."

Defining elements and characteristics of French country decor

Another view of Joyce's dining room.

As Verma explains, "French country is very soft in its details: furniture lines are more delicate, the scale is smaller, pieces take on more feminine shapes, you see curves." While not an exhaustive list, French country style homes often include the following elements: Vintage French furniture, which often features intricate carving, cabriole legs, and is distressed or painted with whitewashed or chalk paint. Consider sourcing antique:

Dining chairs

Hutches

Armoirs

Couches

Patterns such as

Toile

Gingham

Stripes

Plaid

Florals

Elegant accents such as

Chandeliers

Ornate wall sconces

Decorative candlesticks

Muted color palettes like warm yellows, creams, light blue, or soft greens

Natural elements like wood beams

Examples of French country decor

If you're looking to craft French country interiors in your home, consider the following French country decor ideas from Joyce and Verma.

French country kitchen

Crystal chandeliers provide a more elegant touch to what could be described as a farmhouse style kitchen.

French country dining room

A French country dining room designed by Amitha Verma.

French country living room

A sitting room in Joyce's home.

French country bathroom

Joyce's French country bathroom creates a stylish bathing experience.

How to bring French country decor into your home

If French country design feels like the right move for you, Verma and Joyce have tips for helping you achieve the aesthetic. "You've got to have French furniture, because that's really the defining element," says Joyce. She recommends looking for these staples on eBay or other resale websites and local antique shops. She also advises others to look for solid wood pieces with intricate carving, as these embellishments will ensure the country furniture appears true to the era. "Once you have that base, then you can play around a little bit and decide how much you want to stick with the style and how much you want to mix in more contemporary modern elements."

A small dining nook in Joyce's home, which displays a stocked collection of French dishes.

Aside the country furniture, it's important to incorporate a mix of patterns through textiles. "Generally speaking, people are often afraid to use pattern, but that's very French country," Verma explains. She recommends having "at least patterned pillows," though in a full French country home, you'd likely see patterned sofas or side chairs too. Consider throw pillows in a toile fabric, which can immediately add an air of elegance to a space, or a gingham tablecloth, for example, which could play up some of the more rustic elements of the design style. Patterned window treatments are also welcome. For wall decor, the designers recommend embellishments such as vintage clocks or landscape oil paintings. "If you want something really authentic, French dishes and monogram linens are beautiful touches," Joyce adds.

Is French Country outdated?

A vintage chair and buffet in a French country room designed by Verma.

When it comes to home decor, it's common to question the lifespan of a style—especially one that you're considering implementing.

Luckily, while a French country look does include a hearty mix of vintage and antiques, it's not outdated. However, Joyce notes that sometimes the upholstery on the vintage pieces could benefit from a touch up. "Have an upholstery guy on speed dial," she jokes, "send your furniture over there and pick out some beautiful, modern fabric."

Is French country still in style?

Though perhaps overshadowed at times by a classic farmhouse, a French country farmhouse is still very much in style. Outfitted with a modern base and ornamented with antique touches, the style crafts a distinctly timeless feel. Of course, when it comes to any home style, it's always best to embrace the aesthetic that makes you the happiest, not whatever is the trendiest. For those who love a mix of refined decor and rustic comfort, a French country cottage could be just the thing. As Joyce says, "For me, I just think it's so beautiful. It just feels like a warm hug; I feel like your house should embrace you when you walk in, and this style does that."

II. Decoring With Vintage French Decor

Did you already step into a French countryside's home? Then, you may have found yourself captivated by an array of mismatched treasures.

Welcoming, unpretentious and very livable, French country style loves to add antiques that have history and meaning.

Actually, we really think vintage adds charm to any home.

And while we love unique finds, there are a few common denominators in the decor of our French countryside.

So if you ever feel lost when it comes to choose and find authentic French vintage decor & accessories, you'll better read this post till the end!

1. FURNITURE

French country furniture has simple but refined lines, worn wood and paint chipped to perfection.

The French focus on the utilitarian, so the pieces should be functional and comfortable.

But beauty can coexist happily in sturdy, timeless pieces.

Think of the antique china cabinet with its display case at the top, closet at the bottom, and a beautiful patina on the wood. Simple, functional, but also a stunning centrepiece.

2. LIGHTING

Using vintage French lighting in your home creates a link to a time when everything was created with care about each detail.

But don't make your house a palace of a thousand and one tassels. A single chandelier (or two) is enough for the whole house (prefer the living room or the bathroom). Then, put a few wall sconces in your bedroom or in the hallway.

You can also add more simplicity with a table or floor lamp in wood with a linen lampshade for example!

3. TEXTILES

French vintage linens add the right touch of rustic and country that
I love so much.

Antique pieces are beautiful and precious but they were made to be
sturdy, so please don't be afraid to use them!

4. KITCHENWARE

Kitchen is often the favorite room in the house among the French. We love to sit and enjoy lovingly prepared meals with our family and friends.

And we like simple and practical kitchenware which shows charm like ironstone dishes, copper cookware or pottery.

You can't even imagine how many different types of French country kitchen antiques you can collect!

And as they've been used in the past, these old treasures often show a little chip here and there, or a crack. That's what make them unique and will give personnality to your home (I can resist when an ironstone piece that shows a well-worn patina!).

I absolutely love ironstone! I think that's my favorite dinnerware. The flaws tell its story and increase its beauty, especially this so charming discoloration!

You can look for soup tureens, sauce boats, pitchers, bowls or less common pieces!

Transferware

Transferware also mixes beautifully with French country interiors.
I tend to favor floral and geometrical patterns more than elaborate
scenes.

Copper

It's surprising how easily a kitchen can transform with just a few
copper elements.

There are so many lovely old pieces, that can either be flat displayed
or wall hanged.

This adds to the decoration possibilities. And that's why copper has
become one of my favorite kitchenware!

Pottery

I believe that no object evokes Provence better than their glazed pottery, with a yellow, green or blue enamel part.

These pots are just beautiful and obviously fit in perfectly with the French country style.

But we can also find more classic terracotta pots just as charming and perhaps easier to integrate into the decoration because of their neutral colors.

Silver Ware

I'm less drawn to silverware, but it's part of the array we like to
have here in France.

5. ACCESSORIES & ACCENT DECOR

While new accessories can sometimes offer a flair, vintage ones do it without even trying.

Even adding just one or two statement vintage pieces, like a stack of old books surrounded by a pretty lace or a few porcelain door knobs, can instantly give a French country feel to any home.

Old Wood Decor

Think about wooden architectural salvage, bowls, crates, bread boards, sculptures…

You can look for chippy paint and patina.

Metal accessories

There are so many metal accessories you can get for a French country look: lanterns, candle holders, sculptures, balance scales, planters, wire baskets, trays… The list is endless!

Don't worry if they show some flaws or rust, that's part of their story.

Rattan / Wicker accessories

The basket, an undying object! It has been around for hundreds of years.

For a French country look, favor old rattan sneakers or straw market bags. They'll add a rustic touch to your home, while remaining elegant.

Iron accessories

I LOVE antique iron pieces.

The French like iron in the form of planters, antique balance scales,

architectural salvage, sculptures...

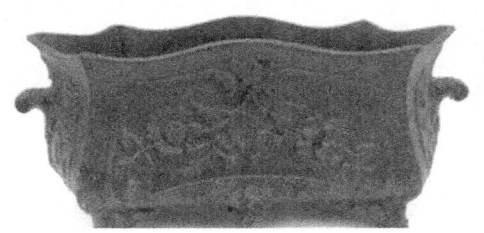

SALE

6. WALL ART

Whether it's a mirror or an oil portrait frame, almost everything in a French country home has an aged look that adds history and charm to the space.

The French like to hang antique mirrors, oil paitings, or old portraits on their walls. To be honest, we don't necessarily like to put pictures of our face on the walls (I don't!). We prefer to show art, collections or one of a kind pieces.

E-mag deco

Maisons de campagne

E-mag deco

Maisons de campagne

E-mag deco

E-mag deco

The most creative also like to highlight single frames within which they can let their imaginations run wild!

E-mag deco

E-mag deco

That's not hard to decorate your home with French wall art. A few pieces are enough. You just need the right frames in the right place.

7. REPURPOSE AND REUSE

The French like to reuse objects, even damaged or incomplete, to do something else. It's a nice way to stand out. Here's some ideas: Salvage the cloche from a cheese dish to showcase small items or flowers.

Vintage Home in France

Add herbs, plants or flowers in your vintage canisters

Put old distressed doors behind your bed to create an headboard.

Use an old bottle holder found in a wine cellar to display bottles but

also tea cups, ball of string, bouquets, or whatever you want.

Possibilities are endless!

III. Vintage French Decorating Ideas

1. French Interior Design

What do I love about french interiors? A lot. Seriously have you seen my home office and my patio makeover?

But I think the core of my love for french interiors is both the versatility/timeless + the glamour. The French love them some gilded stuff, and yeah, samesies.

I love seeing french chandeliers in a traditional American kitchen. French style transcends genres, styles and has a place in any home. (Ok, maybe not a minimalist one...)

You'll sometimes catch me sharing Parisian apartments for sale on my Instagram stories because it seems so chic to live there and be immersed in that gorgeous city. I dream of living in Paris for a year.

Although, to be fair, I would also totally love a french countryside cottage that has a train that could get me to Paris, Italy or any of the other lovely regions around.

I feel like those picturesque cottages have a welcoming look that is the perfect fit if you want to feel like you're on vacation everyday and like maybe, just maybe, my life could be turned into a best selling movie.

2. Vintage French Decorating Ideas

What inspired this post was a little selfish in that it is fun to find images to share, but moreover, I wanted to curate ideas that you could implement in your home.

This way you'll have some items to be on the prowl for when you visit antique shops, estate sales, thrift stores and the like to create your own version of a french country home with vintage pieces.

I know sometimes it is hard and feels nearly impossible to find the vintage item you have your heart set on, so when appropriate I have included some "new" items that have the same aesthetic to make it a bit more feasible.

The ideas below could be taken to create a whole room or space, or you could apply sparingly for a dash of french panache.

French country style and french farmhouse style is so popular, and I adore it, too. While some of the images and decor tips in this post will lend themselves to that type of style, if you love modern french interiors, more Parisian apartment style, more eclectic style, etc. there will be something for you as well.

3. Vintage French Lighting

Empire Chandeliers

A vintage light fixture is high on my list of things I'm always on the prowl for. In fact, a pair of empire style chandeliers are the key design elements of the kitchen island in my forever home. Mallory's kitchen is the perfect example of this. Also take note of the cremone bolts on her cabinets. Spectacular all around.

Brass Sconces

Another example from Mallory is the use of brass wall sconces that add in more of the french vibes. She also uses simple wood pieces in her styling which is an easy way to add warmth for that perfect touch.

Crystal Chandeliers

When also trying to think of french inspired examples of vintage lighting, my mind immediately went to Lory's kitchen. I've pinned so many pictures of her kitchen island in particular because she has these darling mini chandeliers that add so much style.

This is a good example of how to incorporate french touches via lighting in a small space.

Retro Style Lighting

If you lean more modern rather than the feminine baroque style, you could add in retro inspired french sconces above your nightstands. These sconces, while definitely a splurge, are so perfect for this aesthetic.

French Style Table Lamps

I have this thing with lamps, and I can't pass up a gorgeous unique lamp. I have to rescue them all. One of the most iconic french lamps is the bouillotte lamp (pronounced: BOO-lot).

In 2020, I found one that was tarnished to hell, but some Brasso and elbow grease brought it back to life. For $15, this was well worth the price and this is one of my favorite lamps in my home.

Modern French Floor Lamps

A trend I am loving is seeing a very decidedly french apartment clad with the ornate fireplace, soaring ceilings, massive gilded mirror….and then seeing a very modern floor lamp.

I feel some of the common features of these modern floor lamps are a thin base and a wide shade. Almost a little more Italian and mid-century modern, if that makes sense. This one from CB2 would be perfect.

3. French Bedroom Ideas

When you think about it, we spend a lot of time in our bedrooms. I know for awhile there neutral colors and natural elements were all the rage, and we were enveloped in a sea of GRAY, greige and taupe. Now, I see a lot more moody colors such dark greens, maroon, navy and even black. Heck, we had a pink accent wall in our bedroom for three years.

White Walls

Then, I decided a white background was quintessentially french, so I repainted our bedroom earlier this year. I recommend the color Alabaster by Sherwin-Williams as the perfect warm, creamy white if you want a decidedly Parisian backdrop for a bedroom.

French Blue Walls

While I love my creamy white walls, these ever so slightly french blue walls paired with a neutral color palette make me swoon.

Paint Color Tip: Borrowed Light is a great paint color if you're wanting to achieve this look.

I love the lighting in this bedroom, and the addition of the ceiling medallions brings in some ornate to compliment the fireplace.

Tufted Bed

You could go nuts to create a french bedroom with a regency style nightstand, opulent moldings, and vintage inspired linens, but if you want just a dash of french via furniture, I'd opt for hunting down an antique tufted bed like Courtney's.

That might be a tall order to find secondhand, so here's a comparable option for under $500.

Vintage Sheets & Linens

And finally, a french bedroom ideas list wouldn't be complete with mentioning vintage linens.

I often find floral bedding at thrift stores and estate sales for a few bucks, and to me they are useful as well as a timeless decor staple. It's a way to incorporate bold patterns in an easy, inexpensive way. Incorporating some floral bedding mixed with other patterns via throw pillows, duvet covers, etc. can evoke a french country bedroom vibe without going overboard.

If you're not a big lover of florals (first of all, how dare you?!), then shopping for secondhand bedding is easy peasy. Focus on finding quality made linen or cotton sheets in classic white or ivory colors.

4. French Kitchens

At any given moment, I fall between two extremes in terms of what my "dream kitchen" is.

On one end of the extreme, I'd love to live in a french country house where I could enjoy a small, functional kitchen with open shelving to display my copperware.

I'd have wire baskets to hold the produce I bought at the farmer's market. It'd have an aged look with wood beams.

And on the other extreme, I want a kitchen like Randi Garrett's so I can make my peanut butter and jelly sandwiches in style, as the Lord intended.

Cafe Curtains to Hide Storage

The best perk of the rustic style french kitchen is I could do stuff like using darling cafe curtains to hide my cleaning supplies. This would be an easy sewing project (or no sew using hem tape), so keep an eye out for fabric at the thrift.

The dainty brass rod and curtain rings paired with the striped fabric is classic. Also note the plaid cafe curtain on the window.

Copper Kitchenware Accents

When I was trying to french-ify my kitchen and asked for tips on how to do so without painting or anything major, so many people suggested styling with some copper pieces.

In my neck of the woods, copper pieces are easily found in thrift store and antique shops for not much money, and it's an easy way to create a vignette with items you likely have.

Indoor Herb Garden

Every time I look at inspiration for french kitchens, they all tend to have fresh florals or herbs. Finding vintage tea cups, brass planters or even glassware is an easy, inexpensive way to start up a little indoor herb garden.

5. French Living Room

If your husband is like mine, if you state you want a french inspired living room, his mind may go directly to french country decor ideas that he feels are too feminine and frilly OR he may assume everything will be gilded and you'll be living like an aristocrat. So, what do you do?

Bergere Chairs

Incorporate small accents into your transitional home via some accent chairs. Notice how these vintage bergere chairs fit right in amongst the modern art and the Kelly Wearstler lamps.

I've found bergere chairs several times via Facebook Marketplace, so I think with a bit of time and persistence, you'd be able to score some. If not, these are perfect!

Wooden Coffee Table

If you love farmhouse in your own home, or maybe you dig that Restoration Hardware sofa vibe, I'd recommend opting for a french inspired coffee table like the one below.

Definitely buy a coffee table secondhand so you can refinish it or repaint it. This way, it's low cost, low risk.

To keep it french-ish, I'd recommend finding an antique coffee table that has some curves to it, maybe has decorative motifs that could be gilded. I have a whole blog post about metallic paint for furniture to create gold accents and I also have tons of DIY paint guides.

Modern French Coffee Table

A more up-to-date option that is less foo foo would be a modern glass coffee table with a unique silhouette as shown here by Champeau & Wilde.

The juxtaposition of new pieces with old pieces, plus the layering of the colors and animal prints is delightfully unexpected.

Drapery Panels

When thinking about drapery panels, your mind may wander over to the maximalist, tassels, cornice board, valances galore opulence like this:

Well, instead of that think of THIS:

Classic white (or any solid color) pleated drapery panels (measured to perfection via my curtain lengths guide) adorned with vintage tassel tiebacks or add some trim to the edges using iron-on hem tape. Such a perfect way to have custom drapery on the cheap.

Keep an eye out for curtain panels at estate sales in older homes. I've found many a panel that way for nearly nothing and they tend to be very well made.

6. French Decor Accents

Busts & Sculptures

I have a hard time passing up a good vintage bust sculpture if I spot one. I have quite a few, and I will admit I've bought a few new ones from H&M Home and HomeGoods, but nothing beats the old stuff. The antique pieces have more soul, patina and are often more unique.

It's easy to get out of hand with busts. After all, you don't want your house to look like a museum of decorative objects, so I recommend using them to make statements such as this pair flanking a fireplace.

Gilded Ornate Mirrors

David Jimenez' work is spectacular (as is his book), and he's a good example of an interior designer who loves Parisian style but melds it well with more modern approaches.

A vintage gilded mirror is high on my "must haves" list for my home. I've often spotted these on Live Auctioneers, and they can be very affordable in relation to buying a dupe from RH or Anthro.

Trumeau Mirrors

It's my opinion that trumeau mirrors are seriously underrated. We all fawn over the gilded mirrors and their dupes, but a trumeau mirror is opulent yet understated. I once bought one on Facebook Marketplace, flipped it and sold it 4x more and I kind of regret selling it now.

Vintage Candelabras & Candlesticks

Again, you might be instantly thinking candelabra + french= cherubs .

You're not wrong…BUT think on a smaller, simpler scale. Candelabras and brass candlesticks are super hard for me to pass up at thrift stores because they tend to be UBER affordable. I'd recommend buying a bunch, shining them up and using them on a mantle, sideboard, buffet, etc. with other vintage baubles.

French Art

Art is something I am very passionate about and love to shop secondhand for. This is also probably one of the easiest, quickest ways to add in a french vibe.

For the frames, look for beefy, ornate, gilded styles. As far as art goes, I try to find originals that spark interest, feature dutch florals or just flat out have colors and motifs that speak to me.

I have found a few artists I love on Instagram, and their art is definitely worth a look.

French Picture Frames

If you're more of a DIY type, I suggest looking for vintage or secondhand frames at thrift stores, gilding them, and then printing some free museum art for the frame for your own curated collection on the cheap.

Antique French Hardware

Half the fun of DIY home renovations or painting furniture pieces is selecting hardware. I love it all. I love the simple brass knobs, the glass pulls, ornate backplates and all the things in between.

Given how quick and easy it is to swap cabinet hardware (and sometimes door hardware), I thought this category was an important inclusion on this list of vintage french decorating ideas.

Cremone Bolts

Let me preface this by stating finding cremone bolts vintage/secondhand is likely not going to happen unless you go to Round Top or Paris.

But, you can't deny the impact of these vintage inspired bolts. I've been considering hiring a carpenter to make all of my kitchen cabinet doors flush so I could utilize these types of bolts.

Door Knobs & Plates

While on a solo trip to Paris in March 2020 (yup, as the world was shutting down…), I stopped and admired so many darn doors. The intricate design, brass handles/kickplate, and bold hues on a grimy city street made my heart skip a beat.

Antique stores usually have vintage knobs and such, would be great to add some character to your home, but you may want to opt for the <u>vintage look with modern features</u> for easier installation.

Knobs & Pulls

A quick way to instantly change the look of cabinets or furniture is to swap out the hardware. Cabinet pulls and knobs can be as inexpensive or expensive as you'd like them to be.

I often use eBay to find vintage (or vintage inspired) cabinet hardware or escutcheons (a word I will never pronounce correctly). If you love the armoire pulls below, these are pretty similar and affordable.

Brass Gallery Rails

In my dream home, I have gallery rails all over the place, but I love how Alyssa from A Glass of Bovino incorporated them into her bathroom makeover. She has a good tutorial you can follow along with sources.

7. Architectural Details

Brass Open Shelving

Some people hate open shelving, but I love the vintage Parisian bistro vibes that brass shelving with glass shelves adds to a space. You usually see this in black/gold/white, but it also works with a gorgeous blue.

Think of all the secondhand glassware, decanters and barware this type of set-up could hold. Definitely the perfect setting to pour glasses of Veuve Cliquot.

Add Picture Molding

I personally have added so many molding treatments to nearly every room of this house. Not only does adding moldings give any space an air of formality and adds value to a home, it definitely is also a nod towards the "french look".

In our primary bedroom, I went totally girly initially with the pink accent wall and tone-on-tone moldings. I love these ornate molding corners that require no complicated miter cuts to achieve this look.

And in my living room, I did tone-on-tone moldings again, but kept the walls alabaster to allow my furnishings to stand out.

Made in United States
Orlando, FL
27 May 2024

47265214R00049